How To Get a Publishing Deal

(And What To Do If You Can't)

Avril McDonald

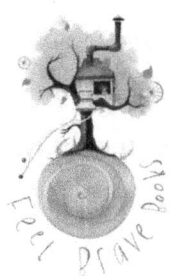

Cover design by Nicola Rowlands (www.nicolarowlands.co.uk)

To all of the people who have helped me on my journey.

AVRIL MCDONALD

Contents

Introduction

I have never been afraid to ask for help. I have received help from so many people in my publishing journey, and for this I am eternally grateful. I think that relationships and collaboration are the key to success if you want to publish a book and make it a commercial success. I don't think you can ever just do it all by yourself.

Now that I have managed to successfully globally publish a series of children's books (and have built a commercially sustainable business out of it), I frequently get asked to help others navigate the world of publishing, which I am only too happy to do because I know how lonely it can feel when you are trying to write and publish a book of any kind.

I think that support and encouragement along the way is critical to help maintain the grit and determination (and often delusional optimism) required to bring it all to fruition. I also think that good ideas need to be nurtured and shaped by others through a 'serve and return' approach to truly flourish.

I surprised myself by getting a publishing deal. I didn't know how to do any of it when I first started out seven years ago. I just had a crystal clear and authentic vision (to create characters and stories to help children manage tough emotions and reach their potential), bucket loads of enthusiasm and determination, and a growth mindset to somehow make it all happen.

I have worked (and continue to work) really hard, and my journey is a testament to the fact that you can learn everything you need to know if you want to. I decided to put all of the answers to the questions that I now frequently get asked into what I hope is a practical and easy to use guide to help others.

My experience thus far has been in publishing a series of children's picture books and an educational teaching guide, so while the information in this book is slanted towards children's publishing, many of the systems and processes included here can be applied across other genres and demographics.

So here it is – my practical, straightforward approach to getting your work published, with or without a traditional publishing deal. Lessons from my own cuts, bruises and successes.

Every publishing journey is different and my strategies might not be everyone's cup of tea, but I hope that this book will give you some insight into the world of publishing and some tools to help you on your way.

1. A couple of useful things to know up front

- Work hard and believe in your creative potential.

- Learn to get comfortable with hearing 'no' as an answer and don't take it personally.

- Listen to feedback from the people that matter (e.g. those who are in or have been in the arena).

- Hold your vision but be flexible with the process and accept that you might have to kill your darlings from time to time.

- If your work really is good enough, the world will eventually see it for what it is and it will speak for itself.

- You can't just have an amazing product, you must take full responsibility for building your tribe (a group of people who believe in and promote your book or brand), and selling it to the world if you want to achieve commercial success from your work.

I don't want to curb your enthusiasm, but it almost takes a miracle to become a successful professional author. The amount of work, grit, determination and luck required is enormous. You might have heard stories about a manuscript being plucked from the 'slush pile' (the stack of unsolicited manuscripts publishers receive) and an unknown author being offered a three book deal with a huge advance, but this is extremely rare.

It is estimated that only around 2% of authors actually make a decent living from their craft, so you need to be on this journey for the love of it (and don't give up your day job just yet!). Have a back-up plan to keep food on your plate during what can be a long and unknown gestation period. The dream of quitting your job to become a writer is unfortunately a reality for only a very small number of writers, but that's not to say it can't happen to you if you really want it to!

Most authors write for five to ten years before they get published. You might have heard of the '10,000-hour rule' (which is that it takes approximately 10,000 hours/five years to become accomplished in a field). To then master the field requires even more hours and experience.

No one will magically make it all happen for you either, you have to do it yourself. And I don't just mean writing the book; I mean marketing it and selling it – even if you've managed to get a traditional publishing deal.

Typical royalty agreements

In a typical traditional publishing deal with an unknown author, the author will get approximately 10% royalties on the publisher's net revenue. So to keep it simple, this means that if the book sells for £10, and the publisher's net revenue from that sale is £5, then the author will get 50p. Out of that 50p the author may have to give a percentage to their literary agent, if they have one (usually 10–15%), and a percentage to their illustrator (which could be anything between 10% and 50%).

This means that an author might be getting only 30p for every book sold. The message here is that you need to sell a lot of books to be able to leave your day job from royalties alone.

If you do manage to sign a publishing deal, that is just the first of many mountains you will have to climb. Once your book is published it then has to sell, and unless you are already an established brand with a huge audience that (unfortunately) doesn't 'just happen'.

But don't let all of this put you off! I'm simply trying to manage your expectations and tell it like it is, so that what might be a huge investment of your time and energy happens for the right reasons. Unless you are incredibly talented, lucky and nail everything the first time around, the journey to profitability on book sales is typically a marathon rather than a sprint.

The great news is that if you can't get a traditional publishing deal, you can still self-publish your work. And if your goal is to create a treasured memoir for your family or turn your stories into something beautiful and real for your children, it can now be easily achieved. Or if your goal is to turn your book into a business or to enhance your existing business, this can also be done – if you are prepared to put in the hard work.

2. Write the book

It's a common notion in the literary world that it is an author's third or fourth book that gets the publishing deal (which you never want to believe when you're starting out). It was my third book that eventually won me my publishing deal so the theory proved correct in my case, and it reinforced the idea that practice makes perfect.

I recommend that you just start now with the writing process – even if you are still trying to crystallise your ideas. The more time you commit to practising writing every day, the greater the opportunity for your ideas to form properly, because I believe that ideas grow from doing, making, trying, testing and pivoting.

We all generally have a lot going on in our busy lives so sometimes it's hard to prioritise writing, but if you have made a conscious decision to publish a book, then you need to make it a priority to fit writing into your day.

If you want to write a book but it's just not happening, (and you are talking about it more than actually doing it), it might be time to re-evaluate if you have truly made the decision. Sometimes we think we want to do something and wonder why it's just not happening, when in reality we just haven't committed 100% to the decision to take action.

In one of my favourite books, The Alchemist by Paolo Coelho, the crystal merchant loves the dream of making a pilgrimage to Mecca so much that he is afraid to actually do it for fear of losing the joy that his dream has brought him for so many years. There is a deep sadness in his failure to act on his dream.

Committing to trying to make a dream come true is scary because it makes us vulnerable and takes us into new places where we haven't been before. I totally 'get' that guy in the crystal shop! I am a dreamer and treasure my precious dreams, but for me the regret of not giving it all I've got to bring my ideas to life has always outweighed the fear of shattering the dream.

As a busy mum, I've done a lot of writing very early in the morning (before the house wakes up) or at insanely loud children's soft plays or parties (where I can completely zone out and get a lot done). You just have to do the best with the time you have.

Talk about your idea to others

Talk to people about what you are trying to do as much as you can (without compromising your intellectual property). Explaining your story ideas to others helps you to get a feel for how good (or not quite there yet) your story might be and will expose areas that you might need to work on or that you haven't completely fleshed out. The more feedback you can get the better, especially in the early stages when you are still crafting your stories. You might also want to join a local writers' circle to get impartial feedback and fresh ideas.

Talking to people also helps you to get insight into the different channels you could potentially go down to further understand your market, subject area and/or build the right networks. It is helpful to start following publishers, bloggers, agents or people of social influence in your target area on social media feeds such as Twitter or Facebook. Share insights with them so that if/when you do ever directly message them and ask for help, they might remember you and be warm and open in their approach to you.

Get clear on your genre and target demographic

Decide on the genre that you wish to write in (e.g. picture book, young fiction) and your target demographic. Publishers want to be very clear on who this potential 'product' they might produce and market for you will be targeted.

If you are writing for children, look up the current general target demographic 'tiers' online and decide where you want to place your work (0–3 years, 4–7 years, 8–12 years, etc.) and invest in the Children's Writers Word Book by Alijandra Mogilner to ensure that the vocabulary you are using is aligned to and will be understood by the age group for whom you are writing. (Although Mogilner's book is US based, it works well as a general global guide.) I think that it's good to expand children's vocabulary by challenging them with new and more advanced words in a story, but there is a delicate balance between trying to expand children's vocabulary and ensuring that the majority of your audience will actually comprehend your stories. Children naturally move at different speeds with their reading levels and there are now more children who speak English as a second language.

Once your manuscript is written, run it through this website: http://read-able.com/ to confirm your independent reading age. This means that you will have a very clearly positioned product. For example, my stories are picture books officially targeted at the 4–7 year age range but they sit at an independent reading age of 10 years. This means that 4–7-year-olds should generally be able to listen and fully understand all of the words and that 10-year-olds should be able to read them comfortably.

Be careful if your intention is to create a piece of work that works across different age groups. I learned the hard way that a book for adults and children, or 'for everyone', doesn't really work. Maybe books like this have worked somewhere but I'm yet to find one. A book needs to be clearly targeted to a single demographic. The first book I produced was just confusing. I took that feedback on board and it became part of the journey that led me to what the stories eventually became and are today.

It's helpful to take a look in bookstores and libraries at books in the genre that you want to write in to get a feel for how they are set out and to then copy that format – for example, children's picture books are usually between 500 and 800 words (no more than 1,000) and the total pages are always divisible by eight (e.g. a 24, 32 or 40 page book).

Keep in mind that a 24, 32 or 40 page book will also include the front and back cover, inside front cover, copyright page and internal title page before your story even begins. Looking at other books of this sort can help you to mock up and plan out your own book.

There are many blog posts and articles on various book genres, but here is a very rough guide to the current genres with some guidelines on expected word count. These guidelines are not set in stone but are simply some general parameters that publishers use. Working within these guidelines demonstrates that you know your genre and market demographic.

Board books: Board books are often marketed as baby, infant or toddler books. They are aimed at the 0–3 year age group. These books are designed to be sucked and dribbled on so the pages are usually made of thick paperboard with a glossy finish. They are usually (but not always) small in size (typically 6 x 6 inches). The length varies but a good guide is 12 pages with 300 words or less. Board books might have a single word on each page or a few very simple sentences. Most board books teach early learning concepts like the alphabet, numbers, colours or nursery rhymes.

Picture books: Large format storybook targeted at the 3/4–8 years age group and usually between 400 to 900 words but no more than 1,000 words in total. They are illustrated in full colour. A very typical size for picture books is 8 x 10 inches. Other standard sizes are 8 x 8 inches (square book) or 10 x 8 inches (horizontal book). In a picture book the illustrations are expected to play an equal part to the text so they should complement one another. Picture books are illustrated using a wide range of media from watercolour, acrylic and coloured pencils to photographs or digital illustrations. A picture book should have a linear plot (no complicated twists) and usually one main character to whom children can relate emotionally.

Picture storybooks: Usually between 900–1,500 words and targeted at slightly older or advanced children. The pictures in a picture storybook aren't as integral as they are in a picture book (e.g. they might appear on every second page to keep the reader engaged) and have more plot development and a higher vocabulary level.

Rebus books: A type of picture book where the illustrations are used to represent certain phrases, words or parts of words. These types of books are great to help children read and understand stories which are more advanced than if they were just text alone.

Easy readers: Aimed at children who are just beginning to read on their own. Like picture storybooks, there are usually illustrations on every other page and storylines are very simple, using basic vocabulary and narratives about common child-like experiences (friends, family, pets, holidays etc.).

Young fiction: Targeted at children in the 5–8 year age group who are just beginning to read independently but are too young to handle full length general fiction. Word counts can range from 1,000 words to 10,000 words. Usually young fiction has both text and illustrations (either colour or black and white line drawings).

General fiction: Intended for children in the 8–12 year age group when they have mastered the mechanics of reading and are now independent readers. These books are considerably longer than the young fiction category (e.g. between 20,000–50,000 words).

Teenage fiction: Aimed at children between 11 and 16 years of age. Not necessarily longer than general fiction (around 40,000 words) but roughly between 50,000–80,000 words.

Adult fiction: Aimed at adults and usually with a word count between 50,000 and 110,000.

Invest in some editorial help

If you are really serious about trying to get a publishing deal, I would highly recommend that you find an editor who deals with your genre/target market who can give you some impartial feedback. It might be helpful to note that some editors might advise more on content while a copy editor will advise more on the text. The lines sometimes blur between this distinction and some will do both.

Good editors are usually best found through recommendations (because there are some bad ones out there!). However, you could start by building up contacts and networks in the publishing industry through your LinkedIn profile and by joining relevant groups or networks. You could also contact the Society for Editors and Proofreaders (www.sfep.org.uk). They have a directory of members, and fairly strict criteria about who can be a member, so there is some assurance of quality.

I find that the best editors are ones who have worked for established publishing houses who now do freelance work, and there are many of those around. To save on costs, you don't have to invest in a full edit of your manuscript (if you have written a novel); you could look at just getting some editorial help on the first chapter to present to publishers with the hope that they want to see more.

Good editorial advice is essential, especially if you decide to self-publish. You can become so close to your work that it's hard to see the areas that need changing, and grammatical/spelling errors are so damaging if they go unseen and you publish your work. Your brain doesn't always read what your eyes see – your brain usually reads what you thought you wrote!

If you disagree with a comment from your editor, make sure that you have a good reason for it. If you are rejecting more than a few of their suggestions, it might be a sign that there are problems – either that the editor is wrong for your book or that you struggle with criticism which could harm your chances of making the best of your work.

Typical editor fees

Editor cost will vary from person to person. I have generally found that an editor will ask how long the book is and/or ask to see it, then will give you costs based on the work they think it will involve. On a children's picture book manuscript (800–1,000 words) I have paid £150 for an amazing four hour working session with an editor, and £80 for another editor to check grammar, spelling and so on. For a longer manuscript, prices will be higher but costs will be case by case based on the editor's experience and the size of your manuscript/amount of work involved. You can generally expect to pay between £20–30 per hour multiplied by the amount of hours they estimate it will take to do the work (your page count).

3. Find an illustrator

If you are writing for children, publishers will often say that they just want to see your manuscript in isolation, and if they like it they will then choose the right illustrator for your content. However, I think it's more powerful if you can go to a publisher with some mocked up examples of your concept and vision for the illustrations.

Even if it turns out that they decide to go with a completely different look and feel with the artwork, I think that it's good to show initiative on the visual elements in your initial approach. You only get one shot, so you need to maximise it and present them with something magical.

I therefore recommend that you find an illustrator before you pitch to any literary agents/publishers. If you can wow them with imaginative visuals and documented evidence that your content and visuals work with children (e.g. a video of you telling the stories to a focus group or some references from your target demographic who are not friends or family!), this will all help to persuade them that you are a creative visionary worth investing in. (For more on focus groups see Chapter 5.)

There are amazing illustrators out there all over the world just waiting to be found on platforms like www.peopleperhour.com (where I found my very talented illustrator who has been a joy to work with and now be in partnership with) and sites like www.elance.com or www.99designs.com. You don't even have to invest in them illustrating a whole book, you can just get a few visuals or a vision board mocked up to bring your ideas to life.

Get as much feedback from your target market on your vision boards/draft illustrations as possible before you commit to an illustrator (e.g. from running focus groups). The visual element is the gateway that draws people to pick your book and discover your content. Getting the illustrations and final design right is therefore critical.

Typical illustrator fees

A first-time storybook illustrator will generally charge £1,500–2,500 for a typical 32 page full colour book. They will most likely charge you 'per spread'. Using a platform like www.peopleperhour.com means that you fully own the copyright on any illustrations you commission.

Once you get a publishing deal (and if you want to continue with that illustrator), you may then have to negotiate a royalty fee agreement (where they get a percentage of your book royalties). If this is the case, then you could negotiate to pay them less per spread up front as an advance on royalties.

I think that an on-going royalty partnership is a good idea because you want your illustrator to get emotionally behind your work. I believe that if you have this type of partnership and emotional investment, it will come through in the illustrations and the whole project will feel like playtime for both of you. But it doesn't have to be this way. You could find someone who is happy to illustrate for a single fee and you own all the copyright. It's up to you.

4. Get clear on your book's market potential

Whether you like it or not, publishing is essentially a complex manufacturing business. Publishing books (particularly books with illustrations) is a matter of art and commerce.

Just like launching any other product into a highly competitive marketplace, it must be authentic, creative, beautiful and/or useful in order to compete with every other product out there. When a publisher is considering whether to sign you or not, they are thinking about all of these things and whether you are going to produce a good ROI (return on investment) for them.

Literary agents are thinking the same thing because they know what publishers are looking for and they know the harsh realities of book sales – their livelihood depends on their potential 10–15% commission from your royalties.

My publishers chose me not only for my concept and manuscript, but also because they knew that I was experienced in sales and marketing, I had identified a gap in the market and I would really use my existing networks and experience to try to sell my work to the world once published. I had a whole business plan built around the books that I brought to the table. This type of roadmap, drive and energy can be attractive for potential publishers and will help you to stand out.

It's critical that you carry out market research so that you can approach publishers with proof that there is a potential market for your book. Go into various bookstores on the high street and read as many books in your genre and for your target demographic as you can. Pinpoint why your book is different and the key unique selling points it will have.

Carry out focus groups, repeat, then carry out more focus groups! If you are writing for children and you haven't engaged in focus groups with children to test and tweak your work, you may be taking a huge risk and could potentially be wasting your precious time. The same applies when writing for adults. If you haven't put yourself out there and tried to get some impartial feedback on parts of your work (e.g. eliciting genuine feedback, responses and engagement from short stories/blogs) then you lack any solid evidence that what you are doing has commercial potential – and a publishing deal is essentially a business investment in a potential product that will sell.

Use as many real-life focus groups as you can to repeatedly test your ideas with the people who matter most – your target demographic. For example, for children's books, use local schools or play groups who are usually open to helping. Children never lie and will tell you exactly what they think, which is what you need (even though you may not want to hear it!). I have always found that the most honest, hard-to-hear criticism was what helped me to make the giant leaps towards my eventual success.

You could organise a little 'focus group party' where you invite your friend's children around and bribe them with some goodies in return for reading and feeding back on your book. World Book Day and other similar annual events are also a perfect opportunity to approach a school to see if they would be open to you coming in and running a story session.

You can never have too many focus groups! Any good product launch goes through rigorous amounts of prototyping, testing, tweaking and redesigning to get it right. A book is no different. You are ultimately trying to create a beautiful product which will be competing against every other beautiful product on the market.

Think about how you will promote and sell your book. You might have a thriving business as a consultant so you are writing your book to complement your business and you therefore have an existing 'tribe' to sell to, maybe you are a speaker and have a good following that you can tap into, or perhaps you can collaborate with someone else with a good audience who might get value out of your work.

You might have the potential to work in schools and get in front of your target audience that way. Just be aware, though, that getting into schools isn't easy and can't be done by everyone. You not only have to have a great product that the children will love, but you also have to be very comfortable dealing with children, holding their attention and engaging their interest.

You also have to get yourself through the school gates, and I don't mean just physically. A head teacher will typically get an average of 120 emails a day from people trying to sell him or her something. You've got to have a really special educational proposition to get invited into the school. This is where relationships are key to get others to help get you in.

You also need a really clever and workable business model to make it work – for example, the school pays for your travel expenses and you don't charge an author visit fee as long as the school agrees to send communication out to parents about your visit, or you charge an author visit fee but donate £1 per book sold to the school. I think it's really important to command the value you deserve for the books and the value an author visit brings to children.

It also pays to try and get a CRB check although as you are never left alone with the children, it isn't always necessary as a guest in a school to have one. It's just another added bonus if you do.

There are many ways to make the money you deserve from your work; you just have to test the water to see what resonates with your audience and understand the value proposition you bring to the table. I don't think schools or parents really understand just how difficult it is to become a successful author or how much investment goes into it. Be careful not to undermine that by underselling yourself. Of course, in the beginning when you are building up your name you need to give a little and try to build trust and value with schools, but as that grows your business models should reflect it. And not just for you but for all the other authors who struggle to put the right value on their creative work and the positive impact it has on children.

You should always be working on building up press contacts and assembling lists of book awards and speaking events that you might be able to get involved with. All of these things will help to boost your credibility when it's time to 'sell yourself in'. People might love your book, but another shift needs to happen for people to actually make a decision to buy your book. Like all selling, it's usually based on relationships and referrals, so the more you can be thinking about this from the outset, the better prepared you will be when the time comes to sell your book to the world. Publishers will want to see that you have a thorough grasp on your book's market potential and some approaches you intend to make to successfully commercialise their investment in you.

5. Traditional publishing deals vs. self-publishing

There are pros and cons of both traditional publishing deals and self-publishing, some of which are outlined below to help you make your decision.

I would recommend that when you are just starting out, your strategy should be to try to get a traditional publishing deal – because they are so difficult to get and give you the kind of potential marketing scale that you could never hope to achieve on your own, unless you are already an established brand/celebrity – while you also plan to self-publish. You can't really lose with this approach.

Some literary agents and publishers claim that if a book has been self-published, a traditional publisher won't want to touch it. However, if you decide to self-publish because you are not having any immediate luck getting a traditional publishing deal, and then manage to get a buzz going and there is proven potential for your book, it might then become an interesting business proposition for a potential publisher. Alternatively, it might prove that it's better for you to continue with the self-publishing route.

If you do self-publish with the hope that you will eventually get a traditional publishing house behind you, think about and provision for a really exciting 'road map' – a clear vision on your next piece (or pieces) of work that will make it potentially exciting for a publisher to back you. There is nothing more valuable these days than having a proven established audience and an exciting strategy for future work.

Traditional publishing deal

Pros:

- Gives you global sales and marketing scale that you could never get yourself (e.g. it's a publisher's job to get you distribution through physical books in stores and through every digital online bookselling platform such as Amazon, Book Depository, iBooks, etc.). Traditional publishers have an insurmountable advantage in the reach of their distribution that a self-publisher will never achieve. Publishers have a dedicated sales force; they might use commissioned sales reps or their own sales reps, or a combination of the two, to cover all of the different regions.

- If your publisher really believes in you, they may invest in a PR company and publicist to represent you. This will give you marketing opportunities that you wouldn't have access to yourself.

- The editing and book production will be 100% correct. Book making is what these guys do. You are guaranteed to have a 'proper' book, produced and launched into the world (without any typos or formatting issues).

- It gives you and your work instant kudos and trust with booksellers and the mainstream market. The publisher signed you so you are trusted as an author, the bookstore puts you on the shelves because they trust the publisher and this all builds trust with your audience. The work on the shelf may be no different to a self-published book, but the perception is that it must be good if it's in a bookshop, and perceptions matter when you are trying to build a brand/audience.

Cons:

- You will likely only get around 10% royalties on your publisher's revenue (e.g. 50p per book if the retail price is £10), which you then may have to split with a literary agent and illustrator. So you need to sell huge volumes just to break even on your investment (unless you sell books yourself and have a good author discount from your publishers which will allow you to make a decent profit per book sold)

- A traditional publishing deal doesn't immediately mean that the publisher will have a large marketing budget for you (or any marketing budget at all!). They may get your book on all upcoming book release lists but they might not have the funds for a great PR launch.

- Some publishers may want to edit or change your work (or want you to use a different illustrator) which can make you feel that you have lost control.

- Traditional publishers have sales teams to get your book into bookstores but that doesn't guarantee that you will get onto the shelves. Book shelf space is at a premium and even well-established authors compete to get on the shelves! It's a bookstore's decision whether they display your work or not, and competition is stiff. Some stores will say they won't stock books if people aren't asking for them – but how can people know they even exist if they aren't on bookshelves? It's a chicken and egg situation that you have to try to get around as a new author. The best way to do this is to get out on your own and work hard to build your audience/tribe.

- It can take a long time to get a traditional publishing deal, by which time you've lost precious time on trying to sell your work.

Self-publishing deal

Pros:

- You have full creative control of your work.

- You potentially have access to a worldwide audience which is incredibly liberating and exciting.

- You have a greater share of revenue on book sales, so if you do things right (e.g. design and market it well) then you have a really good chance of commercial success.

- If you already have a great network or clients that you can sell your books into, you can use your book immediately as a business marketing tool without risking a long wait for a traditional publishing deal (typically one year from signing a deal to book release).

Cons:

- You will not get an advance. You are responsible for (and have to self-fund) your own editorial help, copy-editing, design, pricing, ISBN number (unless you use a platform like Amazon's Create Space or Amazon Kindle Direct where they assign you an ISBN at no charge), printing, marketing, PR, sales, invoicing and accounting.

- Your book won't be on new book release lists so your work will not get into bookshops, and this gives readers a huge amount of trust in the quality of your work. Although you can buy a distribution package through some self-publishing organisations, this often just amounts to being listed in a catalogue. It doesn't mean that you are being sold into stores or getting the same visibility that you would if you were with a traditional publisher.

- You won't receive any coverage in the press. It has become harder to get good press/PR about new books due to the fact that anyone can now self-publish. There is a certain amount of cachet associated with a publishing deal and it helps with credibility when you are trying to get a press article or story published. Doing your own press/PR is not impossible, but you have to work hard at it by leveraging your networks and having a great back story to tell.

6. Signing with a literary agent

Some publishers will accept submissions (otherwise known as your manuscript) directly from an author, but the bigger publishing houses (e.g. Penguin Random House, Hachette, Scholastic, Simon & Schuster) will only accept submissions through a literary agent. Generally, this is because so many people want to publish a book that large publishers simply can't logistically manage all of the submissions coming in (they receive at least 100 new manuscripts a week).

There are three main benefits to having a literary agent:

1. To give your manuscript the visibility of many of the major publishers (who don't accept direct submissions from authors).

2. For the kudos. It's fickle but it's true – an agent gives you some initial prestige as an author. It's the first layer of trust or credibility that can help publishers to believe that you might be worth investing in as an author.

3. To negotiate a better publishing deal than you might be able to yourself.

It's a good idea to try to get a literary agent to represent you, but unfortunately it's not very easy to get one, and even if you do you have no assurance that they will successfully be able to sell your manuscript to a publisher. Much like trying to get a publisher to sign you, to get an agent you need to approach them with your manuscript and a powerful elevator pitch. Networking with exiting authors in your genre and getting them to give you referrals is also helpful.

A literary agent might decide to sign you up and take your manuscript around the major publishers, but if they get a load of no's then they are unlikely to want to sell a second manuscript of yours until some time has passed, for fear of pushing their trusted publisher relationships too much.

I respect and understand this but … your next book might just be the one that nails it (because you learn as you go) and you don't want another gatekeeper potentially stopping your manuscript getting the exposure it needs. The more creative, innovative and clever you can be with your own marketing, the greater the chance you have of getting your manuscript in front of the right decision makers.

I would recommend that you try to get a literary agent while you are also personally submitting your manuscript to any publishers that take submissions directly from unknown authors. This enables you to have irons in every fire and not waste time as many submission processes are typically quite long.

No one will be as passionate about selling you as you will be yourself. If you have the ability to network like crazy and successfully get yourself in front of the major publishers, then go down this route. It's tricky but it's possible. If you have a great vision, passionate intention and bucket loads of enthusiasm, that is contagious and people are usually open to helping you in some way.

Be creative and try to think of innovative, clever and cool ways to get your work/vision/idea into their hands (without stalking them!). If you really want this and genuinely believe in your work, you will be unafraid to do all that you can to uncover every stone in getting the feedback that you need.

I made sure that, in my corporate role, I was always building strong relationships with publishers while I was doing my day job. I also asked all of my trusted business networks for help in what I was trying to do and they connected me with people in the publishing world who I then met for a coffee. Through this I was constantly learning about current trends, who was who, what was or wasn't working and getting a feel for how my work was being received, what was wrong with it and how far I still needed to take it.

If you don't want to get a literary agent and you do manage to get a traditional publishing deal, then it's worth protecting yourself by finding a good copyright lawyer (not a general solicitor) to help you negotiate and close the agreement. It's worth one upfront fee to get a copyright lawyer to do this and give yourself the peace of mind that your work is 100% protected and that you understand all of the terms and conditions. The benefit of a copyright lawyer vs. a literary agent is that the copyright lawyer will ask for a one-off fee and will not then claim any percentage of your on-going royalty payments (literary agents generally take 15% commission on new author's royalties for the rest of the published work's existence).

On the flip side, a copyright lawyer might not have as much knowledge of specific book deals and some of the smaller details that might be easily challenged and/or changed in a publishing contract as a literary agent might, but at least you will have some decent protection and understanding of what you've signed up for.

What if no literary agents want to sign you?

If you can't find a literacy agent willing to take you on this does not need to be a barrier; it just means that you are going to have to work harder to get your work in front of the major publishers that don't accept unsolicited manuscripts. The agents you've contacted may not give you any feedback, but if they do, consider it carefully and tweak your work (particularly if more than one agent gives you the same comments). Agents understand the industry and know what they are talking about; however, they are not publishers, so don't give up just because nobody wants to represent you.

For a new author, if you don't sign with a literary agent, getting the first deal and then building an audience should be the focus. Once you have established this, it will be easier if you later decide to find a literary agent, as they can then help to take you on the next phase of your journey with new contract negotiations and potential new business deals.

7. Targeting publishers and agents

Invest in a book called the Writers' and Artists' Yearbook (it's updated every year) which lists the current details and contacts of all literary agents and publishers and serves as a great guide for writing with lots of helpful insight and resources. I refer to it as a bit of a writers 'bible'. Also very useful are the Writers' and Artists' website (www.writersandartists.co.uk/) and the Writers' and Artists' blog (www.writersandartists.co.uk/blog/).

You can easily go through and filter out the publishers that do not cover your genre and make up a concise contact list of all the relevant/appropriate publishers (and agents) for you to target and approach. As well as the general yearbook, there is also one specifically for children's writers called the Children's Writers' and Artists' Yearbook.

Develop a contact strategy

I would suggest that you set up an Excel spreadsheet and use it to track the progress of your communications with publishers (e.g. the date you contacted a publisher or agent and any actions/next steps). This will ensure that your approach is professional, that you don't accidently contact someone you have contacted already and/or if you get feedback, you know exactly who's who. If you manage to sign with a literary agent who wants to represent you, they will then target any publishing houses that only accept submissions from agents.

Build your networks and have an innovative approach

If you don't sign with a literary agent, use all of your networks and everything in your power to get your idea/submission in front of the major publishing houses.

Be clever, innovative and different in your approach. Talk to as many people as you can about what you are trying to do so that you are on everyone's radar's. Help as many people as you can in their journeys and hopefully you will get help in return.

Monkey bar from person to person to grow your networks as early in your writing process as you can. I have often found that the individual I think might be most helpful to me might not be as valuable as the other people I meet on my journey towards connecting with that person.

There are various effective ways to start building up your

networks: Simply ask for help with honesty, good intention and passion (it's contagious). Most people love to help someone else if the idea resonates and comes from a good place.

Offer your help to new connections. Look for ways that you might be able to connect the dots or add some sort of value to their lives. And if you connect with someone that you hold in awe and are a little intimated by the feeling that you will never be able to give them as much value as they might give you, don't underestimate the importance of what you might be able to offer someone in the future that might just not be clear right now. Or give thanks and honestly say that you can't think of any direct value you might be able to give them back in return now, but that you will 'pay it forward' (which is a lovely and well-respected gesture).

Sign up for Google Alerts in the area that you are either trying to publish in or areas where the people you are wanting to connect with might be hanging out. With every alert, you will find someone new to potentially connect with (either the person who wrote the article and/or people mentioned in the article). Then try to connect with them, referring to the article and asking them for help and/or offer your help to them.

Join relevant groups or associations in your field. Talk to people who are already published about their journeys and who they might know who might help you or recommended channels to go down. Have coffees with anyone you can to try to understand the market and who's who. A big part of getting a publishing deal is being in the right place at the right time or having someone mention you and your work to someone at the right time. Make sure that you and your work are top of mind with all of your networks.

I always think that if I cast 99 fishing lines one will catch a fish. This is also how I view what others might see as 'failures'. I believe that you need to have 99 failures to every one success, so that might be approaching 99 people and having one respond, or testing 99 email subject lines to see which one is your winner. (I mentioned earlier that it's typically a marathon rather than a sprint ...)

8. How to pitch your book proposal to publishers and/or literary agents

Once you have your manuscript and illustrations (if you are writing a children's book) in a simple, easy to access and read format (e.g. Google Slides which are shared, a PDF in folder that sits in the cloud so that it doesn't take up time/space for the recipient to download, or beautifully printed if you are sending it in), you need to prepare to pitch your book proposal to publishers and/or literary agents.

There are two ways to approach publishers:

1. Pitching directly to publishing contacts you have personally made and carefully nurtured during the process of writing your book (e.g. through contacts who have introduced you, groups or networks).

2. Pitching to publishers using their submission guidelines (which are critical to follow if you don't want to annoy them!) as outlined in the Artists' and Writers' Yearbook.

Recommendations on how to pitch

There is advice on how to pitch to publishers in the Artists and Writers Yearbook (and you can find lots of great ideas and inspiration online), but here are some of my top tips to grab attention and hold interest:

Look at books in bookstores in your genre and see who they have been published by. This will give you some good insight into which publishers might be a good fit for your book. Don't just target the 'big five' (Hachette, HarperCollins, Macmillan, Penguin Random House and Simon & Schuster), also think about independent publishers. Research who's who carefully so that you don't miss any opportunities. Independent publishers might be smaller but they may give you the dedicated time you need and be just the right partnership for you at this stage.

Prepare an 'elevator pitch' email. (An elevator pitch is your idea written in such a clear and concise manner that you could pitch it to someone in-between a couple of floors in an elevator.) Although most publishers have very strict submission guidelines (and with good reason), almost every agent or publisher will generally at least look at or accept a query by email or letter. Just be aware that some publishers will never respond to you. Don't take it personally.

Outline in your pitch what your book is about and why you think it will appeal to the masses. Link it to relevant and timely subjects (if appropriate) and/or explain why there is a need for your work or a gap in the market (remember, publishing is ultimately a commercial business).

Remember that you are pitching yourself as well as your book. It helps if you can demonstrate the research you've carried out, the evidence you have that your book will succeed (e.g. focus group videos or results) and how much work you can put in yourself to selling the book should they choose to invest in you (e.g. existing audiences you have access to).

If you have any published articles, have launched any successful projects or had successes that are relevant, mention these to promote your credibility and to show that you have the ability to build an audience/tribe.

Make sure that it's clear from your pitch that you know your audience, and the demographic you are targeting and have carried out due diligence in this (e.g. through focus groups).

Always run a spell check on a pitch you intend to send and also get a pedantic friend (if you have one) to check your work both grammatically and in terms of how well you are getting your ideas across.

Google 'what publishers hate' and you'll get all the information you need on what not to do in a pitch to publishers. The key things this will highlight are not understanding the publisher you are contacting (e.g. sending an adult manuscript to a children's publisher), not being clear on your target demographic/who the book is aimed for, ignoring the publisher's submission guidelines, spelling mistakes, grammatical issues, bad formatting and retelling classic well-known stories.

General responses to expect

You'll generally get one of the mix of responses below from publishers/literary agents:

1. No response (which usually means a rejection).
2. A 'thanks but no thanks' (which is also a rejection but it's nice of them to actually acknowledge your submission and, if you're lucky, you might get some feedback which is rare but not unheard of).
3. A request for a partial manuscript and a synopsis.
4. A request for the full manuscript.

Don't be put off by one or two no's – keep trying and evaluate any feedback you get for patterns as to why your pitch might not be working.

If you don't get any responses at all from your pitch/query, there might be something wrong with it, so it's worth testing a few different versions to see if that helps. If there is still no response, there could be a problem with your proposal in general so you might want to rethink it. If you do get a request for your manuscript, then it's obviously a sign that the proposal is okay.

As a real example of an approach to publishers, below is the email that I sent out to a lot of publishers (that I had already built relationships with and had direct email contacts for) a few days before the London Book Fair that got me my publishing deal:

Hi there!

I have created characters and stories to help kids manage tough emotion and feel brave: www.feelbrave.com (for 4–7-year-olds).
My first book (in a series of books) will be completed in May 2015. The manuscript is attached with some pictures to give you a feel for it. I am interested in finding a publishing/distribution partner and will be at the London Book Fair next week if you would like to meet up to discuss this. I am represented by Bell Lomax Moreton.

I have created a charitable arm (www.friendsoffeelbrave.com) and I am in positive talks to get funding to take the programme into schools which will help educators reach their personal, emotional, social health development objectives.

I also publish parenting articles in mother and baby magazines/websites (attached example of a current article on the shelves in New Zealand). If any of this resonates with you, I'd love to meet up. Or if you know of anyone or channels which may be appropriate, I would appreciate your advice.

I'm not just trying to publish a book – I'm trying to create a movement to bring positive psychology, mindfulness and compassion to the mainstream.

Thanks in advance.
Regards,
Avril

This email is basically saying:

- I've got a website, which shows a strong, clear vision for a future brand that is timely and relevant.

- I've got a manuscript with illustrations that has been tried and tested in the market through my own research and development.

- There is scope for a series and greater business opportunities both in the mainstream and in education.

- I've created a charitable arm with socially conscious aims – I have intentions for my work to serve others.

- I have a literary agent (this gives publishers trust in your credibility).

- I'm writing articles in glossy magazines (more trust – I have something relevant to say/talk about in the market).

9. What to do with 999 no's ...

I remember deciding very clearly one day (after three years of working on my concept) that I was ready to go out and get (what I coined) my '999 no's', and I declared this to everyone I knew – which helped me convince myself to buckle up and prepare for the hard journey and growth mindset that I would need.

I figured that this was a good strategy because I would either get a yes well before 999 no's, or that if I did get to 999 no's then I would know exactly why I didn't yet have a yes and therefore could identify what needed tweaking or areas that I was not strong enough on yet and could go and get some further help.

I don't know about anyone else, but when trying to get a traditional publishing deal, I found most publishers quite scary (and I'm a reasonably confident person). I realise they are constantly bombarded with people wanting to publish a book, so they are used to saying no a lot (and probably get very annoyed with being approached all of the time), and this may explain why I always felt some sort of invisible barrier between them and me. It was as if they were part of an old-fashioned private club of which I would never be able to become a member!

I tried really hard to break down those barriers by being as honest, authentic and connecting in my approach as I could, but it still hurt my ego and felt very isolating when I got cold hard rejections. It also made me feel sad for all of the other writers out there with great ideas who might just need a little nurturing but get a couple of no's, then get put off the idea and give up. (I don't think you ever get it right first pop and it's the nurturing, encouragement and advice that can help to produce someone's greatest work.)

My point is that it's a tough journey trying to get a publisher to believe in you and invest in you. Try to find some good mentors who will support and encourage you if/when you receive a rejection. We are all human, and it can hurt even the toughest of us. It takes a huge amount of resilience to not let them crush your enthusiasm.

Ask any author who has 'made it' and you'll be hard pressed to find anyone who just sailed straight into a publishing deal and didn't have their fair share of knock-backs (unless they were already an established celebrity in their own right, in which case they will have most likely been through their own 999 no's journey in another industry).

A lot of the rebuffs may not actually be so much about your work specifically, it might just be down to bad timing or how your idea is pitched. There is such a huge amount of amazing work out there that you could be as talented as any of the current best-selling authors, but when promoting any idea in such a competitive and saturated environment, it's about cutting through and getting the right people's attention at the right time.

If you get a few no's, keep trying other publishers and agents (what one publisher hates, another may love). If you're getting quite a few, it's probably time to think about rewriting and carrying out some focus groups (if you haven't done them already) to really make sure that your target demographic are giving you positive feedback. If you get a lot of no's, it might be time to go back to the drawing board and turn the idea completely on its head, using and acting on all of the constructive feedback you can get.

I got my fair share of rejections so I decided that I was going to self-publish while I continued to work in parallel to get a traditional publishing deal. I happened to have won a mentoring session with the UK's number one parenting author, Annabel Karmel, and she introduced me to a few of her contacts (which is how I found my poetry coach and editor). She also strongly advised me to attend the London Book Fair.

Now, you can't just show up at the London Book Fair and try to get a publishing deal with some random unsolicited approach – publishers are generally there to meet business partners and share ideas – but what you can do is try to secure a meeting before the fair with literary agents or publishers, and this is what I did.

By the time the London Book Fair had come around, I had a lot of great publishing contacts and I had been given the name of a good contact by Annabel who was willing to meet with me and share his wisdom. By this stage I had a completed manuscript with illustrations (that I had self-funded), I'd managed to get an article published in a glossy magazine about children's mental health and I had set up a charitable arm, so I had a reasonably good story about my vision and roadmap for growth.

A few days before the London Book Fair, I emailed every good publishing contact I had (with the example email from the previous chapter) telling them that I would be at the London Book Fair and would they like to meet to discuss either a publishing deal or a distribution deal. (A distribution deal is when you produce the book yourself but a publisher agrees to sell it using their existing distribution arms and sales teams.)

It turned out that the publisher which wanted to sign me was one that I hadn't approached before. They were looking for a crossover author who could sit in both the mainstream and in education. Our successful partnership was born, and within eight months we launched the 'Feel Brave' series of books and an educational teaching guide.

I think it's important that you embrace the no's as part of the journey and find a balance between trying understand why they said no (to get constructive feedback on areas that you might want to tweak) and being able to accept that if you knock on a door and it doesn't open … it's just not your door! Every no helps you get one step closer to your yes.

10. You've signed a traditional publishing deal – what happens next?

If a publisher offers you a publishing deal, I would recommend that you take it, but before you sign on the dotted line make a last minute call-out to other publishers telling them that you have had an offer and do they want to have the opportunity to also consider your work before you sign. It's a nice situation to be in if you have a publisher bidding war over your work. It's rare but not impossible. Dream big!

As an unknown author, you are (unfortunately) not worth much to a publisher (again, don't take this personally, it's just fact), and therefore have very little room to negotiate. If you haven't got an agent, you could try to get one now (a publishing contract offer can make it easier to find an agent) and take their advice. Push back on anything that is a complete deal breaker for you, but keep in mind that pushing back on too much, or causing too many delays in the process, could risk them withdrawing the offer.

Publishers might offer you an advance on future royalties or they might not, as you are an unknown author and therefore a commercial risk to them. Many books that publishers invest in barely cover their costs or just earn a marginal profit so publishers need to keep their costs down. Advances are often calculated at a half to two-thirds of what the publisher expects to earn from the book, so if a book is projected to retail at £10, and the publishers get a net profit of £5 per book, a £5,000 advance would mean they are expecting to sell at least 2,000 books in total.

Publishers generally sign a deal at least 12 months before the book is released and will want to have the finished manuscript ready for editing 9 to 12 months before the publication date. Publishers have many deadlines to meet before publication (e.g. editing, book design, marketing plans, bookseller's catalogues, sales briefs).

For an unknown author, the first print run might be only 1,000–2,000 books. Publishers need to test the water and not risk a huge print run until they can get a feel for how the market is receiving the book, how much publicity it is getting and how initial sales look.

Publishing houses are a business and times are tough. They may or may not have a marketing budget allocated for a PR company/publicist in the run-up to the book launch. As an unknown author you can't just write the book and expect them to do everything. Like all business models, it's all about shared risk and reward. They will invest as much in you as they feel they might gain from you/your brand/your product, and it's a team effort to then make it work. In most cases, you will have to do a lot of the marketing of your book yourself (even if your book deal is with a large publishing house).

A publisher will give you the potential global scale that you could never achieve yourself (e.g. get you on newly released book lists), but you have to sell yourself and do all you can with your publisher to get the books to sell in the quantities you need to reach a tipping point. You don't have the luxury of hiding in your writer's cave while someone else sells the book for you. You've got to come out and try to build and maintain your trusted tribe/audience.

A publisher will only do so much to market and sell your book, however, and if it is not showing positive signs in selling then there is a risk of them loosing hope in you and the print runs drying up. This is why it's so important to really build your relationship with your publisher and work as hard as you can to sell your books. Publishers should give you a decent author discount so you should be trying to make your own business out of that by setting up an online shop and promoting yourself, doing events and/or innovative marketing campaigns into your targeted areas (e.g. school author visits, corporate speaking events, book signings).

You should also make sure that you have the option to be able to sell your books yourself at a good author discount (e.g. 50% discount on RRP, in which case you can get out there and sell your own books and make a decent profit of say £5 per book). This is where you have the best chance of turning your writing into a commercially sustainable business, but you need to get out there, be 'present' and do that sales groundwork yourself. No one is going to do it for you and the sales work is one of the hardest part of the process.

If your publisher can see that you are making good in-roads, and are a profitable sales channel for them, then they will be more likely to be open to investing in marketing campaigns with you. For example, you could offer to manage a marketing campaign with them if they will provide a certain number of books (e.g. if schools are your target market, get your publishers to make up a flyer and send out a sample book to some schools to promote a potential author visit). Manage the campaign for them by recording the details and following up with the schools to see what the feedback is and what the return on their investment was to potentially run more of these types of marketing campaigns in the future.

Make up marketing target lists and test as many different approaches as you can (e.g. different offers, different tones in the way the offer is presented and test different subject or email header lines). Try to get as many author visits and/or speaking opportunities as you can in areas or groups that are relevant to your target demographic. Look at creative ways to get others to help you (e.g. find a friend who is happy to help you by building solid prospect lists and emailing target customers and give them £1 for every book that they sell).

How the editorial process works

Your publisher will either have in-house editors or will work with a range of freelance editorial consultants, but you might want to personally invest in a little extra help before it gets to that stage.

I knew the exact editorial profile that I needed for the 'Feel Brave' children's books and knew that any publisher that I managed to sign with would be unlikely to have this type of person as a regular editorial consultant. I needed an established published poet, and I managed to find that person myself through a lot of networking and asking for help.

The best advice my editor ever gave me and that I always share was to remember to give a 'gift' to the reader every page or every few couplets (if you write in verse). A gift is something that warms the heart or makes us laugh – for example from my book The Grand Wolf:

They'd go for long walks where they'd talk of great things
Like how forest fairies dry out their new wings.

I try here to give two gifts. The first gift is where they 'talk of great things' which aims to give a feeling of ancient wisdom to the precious conversations they obviously share. The second gift is the suggestion that fairies might have to 'dry out their new wings' like a beautiful butterfly does. The aim is to add a whimsical note to the types of conversations they would share together on these special walks, which will perhaps take the reader to a memory of walks and talks they have shared with someone they love.

Get clear on your book's product roadmap and launch plans

Get as involved as you can in understanding exactly what your publisher plans to do for the launch of your book, both practically on the roadmap to launching the product and from a marketing/sales perspective.

The more you can work on it as a team, the better the potential to get the right exposure. Share your networks and contacts and pull on your strengths in areas where you might be able to enhance the marketing strategy.

11. You're going to self-publish – now what?

Self-publishing is going through a renaissance. It used to be considered a bit of a 'vanity' thing to self-publish your own book but now it's a very credible option to get your work out into the world without the limitations of (what used to be) the big publishers who previously held the key to any writer's success. It's an exciting time to be a writer!

There are quite a few good platforms available now to help you self-publish, and whatever you need to find out about how to do it you can discover by googling it online and finding forums or FAQs. Any questions you have will most likely have been asked (and answered) by someone else, so with time and patience you can pretty much work it all out by yourself.

A great podcast show I would recommend you take a look at is http://self-publishing-journeys.com by Paul Teague where many answers to questions about self-publishing and handy tips/ideas can be found.

The whole self-publishing process can be quite daunting, but if you have hired a designer to help you with your book cover, they should be able to help you make sure that you have the right cover template/format for the cover of the book you are self-publishing and most self-publishing platforms either have templates for you to use to upload your manuscript/content or very clear guidelines on formats.

Some popular current self-publishing platforms are:

CreateSpace

CreateSpace is owned by Amazon and allows you to print books for free from anywhere in the world (upfront or print on demand). You'll still have to pay for an independent editor and cover design, of course, but the CreateSpace process is essentially free in return for a revenue share on future sales (Amazon take approximately 40% of your retail price plus a fixed charge and per page charge – you can find out all about their business models on the CreateSpace website in the 'understanding royalties' section). The only catch with CreateSpace is that it doesn't automatically include distribution of your books to all major distributors (e.g. Ingram). In order to do this, you will be charged a fee for an expanded distribution package. You can use a free ISBN number from CreateSpace but if you wish to then print your book yourself and sell it, you can do this but you need to buy your own ISBN number in order to do so.

Kindle Direct Publishing

Kindle Direct Publishing is also owned by Amazon. It enables you to publish your book at no charge electronically (as an e-book) on Amazon for Kindle (an e-reader exclusive to Amazon) from anywhere in the world. You receive a 70% royalty on the retail price of your e-books sold through Amazon Kindle Direct (unless you are outside the territories that Amazon list as being included in this royalty option, in which case you receive a 35% royalty).

Bookbaby.com

BookBaby will publish your e-book and/or offer you print on demand but they do have an upfront fee. I published my first e-book using BookBaby and found the process really easy and user friendly. I also like the customer support they offer, which is good if you are new to the process and a little afraid of how to make it all happen. BookBaby compare their service against their competitors on their website, which is useful to for making comparisons. They also compare royalty payments to help you make your decision on which platform is best suited for you as a self-publishing partner.

Kobo

Kobo is an e-book retailer and is also the name of their reading device. If you choose to upload your book to Kobo, it means that it will only be available on Kobo. However, it can be uploaded from anywhere in the world.

Draft2Digital

Draft2Digital is a distributor which will upload your e-book across other retailers such as iBooks (iTunes) and NOOK (Barnes and Noble), Kobo and a couple of other sites that are not as well known. In some countries, iBooks and NOOK don't allow you to upload your book to their platforms because they do not accept bank accounts from all countries. If you do live in one of these countries, it would pay to use a provider like Draft2Digital to give you exposure on these platforms (and payment from them). One of the key things about Draft2Digital is that they do all of the formatting of your manuscript! You just provide them with a Word file and they will do the rest.

Some things to be aware of

Be wary of any companies that take a large upfront fee to help you self-publish your book (aka vanity publishers), unless you purely want to get your book made for the fun of it or to give to your family and friends. If you use one of these companies, you can end up paying a lot of money for broken promises. A great website which will help you understand the risks of vanity publishers is www.vanitypublishing.info/.

Before you self-publish, try to get feedback on your book (content, artwork, typeset, cover design, etc.) from someone in the business. Don't rely on friends and family for this as they are likely to be biased and are probably not in the book market. Ask a few local booksellers/book buyers. They might not tell you what you want to hear, but it could be the difference between producing something that is commercially viable and something that just won't sell.

Find yourself some good quality editorial help

Editorial help (I think) is highly underrated. As I mentioned in Chapter 3, a good editor will know so much more about writing and the marketplace than you do and will give your book the professionalism it needs. It's well worth the upfront investment, especially if you are self-publishing.

12. How to do your own PR and marketing

It's not enough to just create an amazingly beautiful product. You have to market it and sell it yourself, with or without a traditional publishing deal.

With a traditional publishing deal, you will have the benefit of your publisher's existing sales and marketing efforts (however big or small the budget is for you), but you still need to do a lot of your own sales and marketing work to enable you to get good sales momentum on your book.

If you choose to self-publish, you will have to do all of your own PR and marketing, so it's good to start laying those foundations and building up your networks as soon as you start writing.

Use LinkedIn and start with contacts who might help you in the initial stages. I would highly recommend that you purchase the LinkedIn Premium package. It costs around £120 a year, but I think it's invaluable in terms of the number of contacts it helps you to build by being able to search for and find the right people and send connection requests to them.

Monkey bar from contact to contact and make new connections using well-thought-out approaches. It's okay to send a request for help to someone and it will be well received if you've done your research on them and have a clear logic as to why you are asking for their help.

Most people really enjoy helping others if and when they can. What's nice is if you just start connecting with people by telling them what you are trying to do, explaining why you want to connect with them and simply asking if they would be so kind as to recommend any good channels that they think you should go down or people/organisations that you should contact.

Try to get as much press as you can

Good press is vital. If your publisher invests in hiring a PR company and/or a publicist, that's great, but make sure you are across everything they are doing so that nothing falls through the gaps.

A PR agency is likely to be working on a set fee to promote you. They will not have a share of future royalties, and naturally they won't be as passionate about the potential of your work as you are, so try to stay aligned with what they are doing to constantly check that no opportunities are being missed.

How do you do this delicately? Build a really good relationship with your publicist and try to help them do their job as well as they can by asking the right questions, adding your own suggestions and exploiting your networks to enhance the overall PR plan.

Set up an Excel spreadsheet and start developing your universe of contacts to approach to get a story (but always align these with a publicist if you have one so as not to step on each other's toes). Remember that a story is all about giving the audience some 'value'. Find and connect with bloggers in the area in which you are writing. Bloggers are always wanting good content so link up with them and propose a story which will be of interest to their readers.

Really good PR is when you put out a great story and the reader likes it so much that they then become curious to find out more about you and potentially want to buy your book: 'Here's a great story or some information that is going to add value to your life. Oh, and by the way, I've written a book …' It's a pull (not a push) marketing technique.

If your book has a clever idea attached to it or important subject matter, try to build stories around this hook. For me, a lot of my own personal story (growing up with anxiety) has been a big part of my books, so there have been a lot of great angles in writing about that and giving parents/teachers strategies to help their children cope with tough emotions.

Be bold and approach TV stations and national newspapers. You have nothing to lose! If you can craft a good story or help give exposure to relevant and timely subject matter, then you might just have an interesting and timely perspective they are looking for. If anything, you will be starting up a relationship with them that you may be able to call upon later when you have built more of your story and/or audience or a key date comes around that is relevant to your work that you can then jump on.

For a new author, great press doesn't always immediately convert into sales so be ready for that. What it does do, though, is to develop credibility for your future sales efforts. If you start a very targeted email campaign, for example, and your website has some great press, you achieve instant trust in the first two seconds that someone might give your website/brand/work to prove itself. (Generally, we make decisions about a brand in a short amount of time so start thinking about how you would like that user experience to be and develop it with that in mind.) If you get a decent amount of press, have very clear links to those publications and articles on your website so your audience can see them.

The importance of a great website and good social media channels

It's critical to have a great website either on your subject matter (if it warrants it) or just as a personal branding website. I use www.wix.com for all of my websites and can't recommend them highly enough. I find them very simple and intuitive to set up and great to start with on a free model and then grow with as your work develops.

A great website means you have somewhere to direct people to and to showcase your work and your brand. Get a designer to help with any logos and branding to give it a professional look. You can do this at very reasonable rates using the platforms such as www.peopleperhour.com and www.upwork.com.

Create a Facebook page and Twitter account for your book/brand too and start working at getting people to follow you sooner rather than later. A good way to get noticed on social media channels is if you can get a picture with a celebrity or an influential person in your field, so grab any chance you get to do this! As long as you ask with good intention and honesty, it can really help to spread awareness. Try to test different articles, videos, pictures to see what resonates or gains interest on a regular basis. Learn from these experiments so that over time you are developing your brand's 'voice' which will help you to build your tribe.

Reid Hoffman, the founder of LinkedIn, once said, 'If you're not embarrassed by the first version of your product, you've launched too late.' I love this quote because it's a reminder that we all have to start somewhere with our product, website, book or brand, and we usually start a long way from where we are going to finish (or it turns into something that we never expected). The earlier you start, the faster you'll evolve it into what it needs to become to be embraced by the world.

Selling your books

When my books launched in June 2016, I excitedly (naively) asked a lead buyer of a national bookstore chain in my native New Zealand (where I had achieved amazing press support across all media channels) if they would support me by stocking my books across their stores. She bluntly said, 'No – no one is asking for them.' It was then that I realised that I was going to have to build my brand myself so that eventually, one day, people might start asking for my books in bookstores.

This also made me appreciate that bookstores may not actually be the most efficient place for me to start – I might be banging my head against a brick wall. I tried some alternative routes – for example, I can now go into schools and sell up to 150 books at a time. I'm less concerned about bookstores now; they are just a 'nice to have' once you've established your brand.

When it comes to selling your books (much like sales across all industries), it all comes down to relationships and networks. When it's time to sell, you should have a great long list of contacts – relationships you have been nurturing from day one – to ask for help.

Develop a list of potential organisations or groups who are good sales prospects and start contacting them and building a relationship. Get out and about as much as you can in front of your customers (e.g. school visits, speaking events, conferences), selling your books and talking with your audience to better understand your market, their needs and your competition.

It's a long road to making a commercially sustainable business out of your writing. It takes determination, hard work and constant testing. Trial different email subject lines, different sales angles and different pricing models (e.g. if you are speaking at events or going into schools) until you see it working. Relentlessly apply for grants (where appropriate), enter book competitions and propose author visits to meet your customers and grow from the ground up. Start where you find yourself and work your way up.

Helpful podcasts and creative marketing ideas

There are some helpful and inspiring podcasts that can feed you with ideas and practical strategies around sales and marketing. Some of the best I've listened to are from Jay Abraham with his 'Ultimate Entrepreneur' podcast show and Tim Ferriss' 'The Tim Ferriss Show'. Tim dissects the strategies, behaviours and patterns of effectiveness of successful thought leaders so that you can model them yourself and reap the rewards. There are so many great creative, innovative ways to market your work and grow your audience if you just keep your ears and eyes open to them.

My overall favourite thought leader in the science of achievement is Anthony Robbins. His view is that you can pretty much achieve anything you want in life if you just find someone who's doing it well already and ask them for their recipe. Listen to or read any of his work and it will really help across all areas (professional and personal) of making a commercial success out of your creative work and, most importantly, to ensure that you are personally enjoying the journey.

Try to get some marketing help if you can. Once you have a book, you should have some fat to play with in your profit margins (e.g. from your author discount with your publishers) to allocate to marketing (e.g. if your book retails at £10 and you can buy it with an author discount for £5, you could allocate £1 per book sale to a marketing commission). You might find someone who is willing to have a go at doing some direct marketing email campaigns for you on a commission basis.

Get creative to get the help you need and you may well produce a win-win situation. Jay Abraham has some amazing tried and tested ideas in this area that are well worth a try.

13. Some final personal learnings

I was thrilled to find out that my books were in one of London's largest central bookstores, so I passed by one day to take a look at where they were positioned (and maybe secretly just leave one or two strategically situated where all eyes could see them!).

However, when I arrived I found they had unfortunately been categorised in the education section on the top floor rather than taking pride of place in the children's section. This made sense because I have also written a teaching guide and this store had bundled them together in education, but I knew that the children's books were totally lost up there.

I informed the retail assistant and she graciously told me to take the set down to the children's department for them to be re-categorised. I laughed to myself as I walked them over to the children's section realising how much of a hands on author you need to be until you have reached your tipping point, with a large trusted audience and comparative book sales.

As I mentioned in Chapter 2, the publishing deal is just the first mountain you have to climb and that takes a growth mindset and a particular combination of talent, grit and resilience. To follow that up with the right PR/marketing, and then convert that into book sales, takes a whole other set of skills. You have to be really present and build your book/brand from the ground up – grass roots style.

Making a commercial success as an author is much like making a success of a start-up business – you need to roll up your sleeves, take responsibility for everything initially and have a huge amount of passion and energy. It's an especially lonely journey if you self-publish because you are making all of the decisions, no matter how many coaches or mentors you might have.

When someone with no connection to you whatsoever buys your book, reads it and loves it, it makes all that work worthwhile and is a true sign of success.

During my own publishing journey, I have fought hard to bring my books to life, and now I am fighting tooth and nail to get the world to embrace them. The journey can feel like it gets harder with each step, but like most challenges, the harder it gets, the greater the satisfaction with the successes and wins.

Juggling a family at the same time has felt like trying to walk down a road while having tomatoes thrown in my face! It's a constant sell: selling to publishers to invest in you, selling to the audience to make a buying decision in a highly competitive and overcrowded market and selling to your family to allow you the time necessary to do it all.

Writing is such a wonderfully creative and cathartic exercise in human expression and I believe that we all have great stories to tell. There has never been a better time to transform your own ideas into a reality, so I wish you all of the creative spirit in the world to enjoy the journey as much as I have and continue to do.

About the author

Avril McDonald is the author of the 'Feel Brave' series of books (little stories about big feelings for 4–7-year-olds) and founder of Feel Brave (www.feelbrave.com). Avril is an ex-primary school teacher, businesswoman and mum. She is also a fellow of the RSA (www.thersa.org) which has a mission to enrich society through ideas and action. Avril is from the Kapiti Coast in New Zealand but currently resides in the UK with her partner and their two children.